IRISH RAILWAY IN PICTURES

No. 4
The Giant's Causeway Tramway

by

Michael Pollard

Crest of The Giant's Causeway, Portrush and Bush Valley Railway and Tramway Co. Ltd.

(Michael Pollard)

This was carried on a few powercars and trailers as most did not have a suitable panel on which to display the crest. It is seen here on the side of saloon No. 2, now preserved at the Ulster Folk and Transport Museum, Cultra. It gives the Company name in full and offers an artist's impression of the famous Causeway. The two strolling visitors are enjoying the sea air and the view; no doubt a hidden message that people might see themselves in the picture also and take the tram to achieve this happy state.

Published by
Irish Railway Record Society, London Area
3 Amelia Court, 45 Highland Road, Bromley, Kent, BR1 4AE

Introduction

It is very fitting this memoir of the Causeway Tram should be produced to mark the opening of the Giant's Causeway and Bushmills Railway on part of the same site. I am delighted to know of the continuing interest of so many people in the pioneering work of my forebears, Dr Anthony Traill, F.T.C.D., and William Atcheson Traill, M.A.(Ing.). It is a pleasure to thank the London Area of the Irish Railway Record Society for producing this excellent publication.

Richard Traill
Bushmills, Co. Antrim

Historical Introduction

The Giant's Causeway, Portrush and Bush Valley Railway and Tramway Co. Ltd. (to use the Tramway's full company title) was the brain-child of two brothers, William A.Traill, a civil engineer, and Dr Anthony Traill, a scientist and Fellow (he became Provost in 1904) of Trinity College Dublin, members of a well-known family in the district.

Railways were introduced into Ireland in 1834 and by the 1860s, most major towns had been connected to the rail system. Portrush was reached in 1856.

Portrush was a port and a holiday town, being eight miles from the world-famous Giant's Causeway. At this time, the only connection was by horse car. The two brothers saw this as an ideal opportunity for the formation of a tramway to connect Portrush to the Giant's Causeway and, following two earlier unsuccessful attempts by others, launched their scheme in 1879.

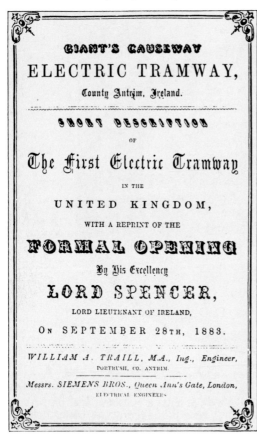

Front page of the reprint programme for the Opening in September 1883.

W.A. Traill, M.A. (Ing)
(Author's Collection)

William Traill was employed by Her Majesty's Geological Survey of Ireland and so was aware of the extraction of iron ore from the hills of north Antrim and its export to England. Mr Traill saw his tramway as a means of transporting ore to the harbours at Portrush and Larne by his associated light railway from Bushmills to Dervock on the Ballycastle Railway, hence the inclusion of the words 'Bush Valley Railway' in the title. The link to Larne was to be completed by a proposed connection to the Ballycastle line near Dervock, from Rathkenny on the Ballymena, Cushendall and Red Bay Railway. If completed, this would have created a 48 mile narrow gauge connection from Larne Harbour to the Giant's Causeway, instead of the 85 mile journey by 5ft 3in gauge railway and road - a fascinating 'might have been'.

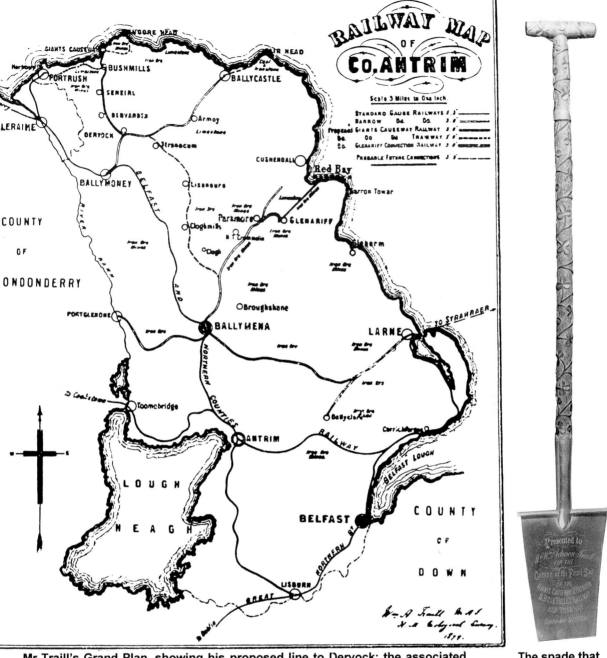

Mr Traill's Grand Plan, showing his proposed line to Dervock; the associated line connecting the Ballycastle Railway to the Ballymena, Cushendall and Red Bay Railway; so completing a shorter narrow gauge route to Larne Harbour.
(Courtesy Ulster Folk and Transport Museum)

The spade that was used to cut the first sod.

The project was intended to be in three parts:
  1   A roadside tramway from Portrush to Bushmills.
  2   A light railway from Bushmills to the Giant's Causeway.
  3   A light railway from Bushmills to Dervock on the Ballycastle Railway.

The gauge of the line was to be 3ft to allow for the connection with the Ballycastle line at Dervock.

The two brothers had lived in Ballylough House, which was located adjacent to the River Bush, some two miles south of Bushmills. Their imagination may have been fired by the use of water power in the old flax mill at Walkmills nearby and its potential to drive a dynamo to generate electricity, which was in its infancy at that time.

They organised a public meeting in October 1879 to support the formation of the line and deposited a Bill before Parliament which received the Royal Assent in August 1880, allowing their proposed line to proceed.

The Act of Parliament had received considerable opposition both from the local Grand Jury and a local landlord, Sir W.T.MacNaghten, who was concerned that the Bushmills to the Causeway section of the line proposed to cross the drive to his home, 'Dundarave'. He dropped his opposition, when this section was withdrawn from the original Act. This left the brothers with little local support for capital investment. However, they had wealthy and influential friends and, at a meeting in Trinity College Dublin, the capital of £20,000 was subscribed.

William Traill then pointed out the potential for the generation and use of electricity for the Tramway to Dr William Siemens, brother of Werner von Siemens who had first demonstrated a short electric railway in Berlin in 1879 and later at the Crystal Palace in 1881-2. Dr Siemens subscribed £3,500 and became a director of the newly formed company. His own London-based company, Siemens Brothers, became electrical engineers to the Tramway.

Experimental work, by Dr Edward Hopkinson of Siemens, commenced immediately using a 25hp steam engine at Portrush. At this time, the longest electric line was just a mile and a half long at Lichterfelde in Germany, using the two running rails for the electricity supply. Experiments at Portrush showed that the two-rail system would not work on this line, especially in wet weather, as insulation was unreliable. The only obvious solution was a third rail and this was placed on the trackside at a height of 17in above the ground.

A power station was constructed on the site of a former flax mill at Walkmills using two turbines, each of 45hp, driving a 40hp generator. The head of water was 26ft and the flow of water was controlled by an operator opening and closing the flap valves on the top of the water tubes feeding the turbines.

Since the Board of Trade had forbidden the use of the third rail in the urban areas of Portrush and Bushmills, the Tramway bought two steam engines to haul the tramcars from Portrush Station to the depot on the outskirts of the town and for the 'branch' at Bushmills to the market place. The line was inspected and approved in January 1883, allowing steam operations to commence, but it was not until September that the problems of electric transmission were overcome.

Opening Ceremony 28th September, 1883. *(Author's Collection)*

The official opening took place on 28th September, 1883. Mr Traill invited many European dignitaries, including Queen Victoria and the German Emperor, but they declined. The line was opened by The Lord Lieutenant of Ireland, Earl Spencer, Great Grand Uncle of the late Princess Diana. At the time of opening, the line only ran from Portrush to Bushmills, but after a further Act of Parliament, the extension to the Giant's Causeway was opened in July 1887.

The line, which had been running with steam since January 1883, did not commence regular use of electric operation until 5th November of that year. Steam engines still operated in Portrush and on the Bushmills branch and, at busy periods, hauled trams along the whole length of the line.

By the mid 1890's there had been many accidents with the third rail, including the death of several animals. Matters came to a head, however, in August 1895 when a cyclist hit the kerb at the side of the line, fell on the third rail and died shortly after. The inquiry following the accident ruled that the voltage of the third rail was to be reduced from 250 to 225 volts - effectively only allowing one tram to operate at a time.

A decision to install an overhead line system, at 500-550 volts, was taken in 1896 and the work was completed in July 1899. Walkmills power station was re-equipped with a new generator in 1901. Two new turbines of 75 and 60hp were installed in 1900 and 1903, and in 1907 a new 550 volt generator of 130hp output. In 1911 an auxiliary electric generator, powered by a gas engine, was installed at the Portrush depot. The plant was to provide power when the water levels in the River Bush were low.

In 1899 and the following few years, four new 'toast rack' powercars were obtained, which were to become the mainstay of the fleet, with one of the old saloon powercars being fitted with a new chassis, motor and overhead equipment.

The line was often short of power and depended on steam locomotives to supplement the electric cars at busy times. Following the First World War, traffic was busy and the steam engines became worn out. A decision to upgrade the power plant at Portrush was taken and in 1925 a new 132hp oil engine driving a similar generator to that at Walkmills was commissioned, the opening ceremony being held in July 1925. The two generating plants could not work in series, due to voltage variations at Walkmills, so at busy times the overhead line was split at Dunluce.

In 1937, a tramcar was purchased from the recently closed 3ft 6in gauge Dunfermline system. It was a double-deck tram and had a chassis similar to the existing powercars. The top deck of the car was removed and the chassis re-gauged to 3ft, after which it entered service in June 1938, as No. 24. This brought the total number of powercars to six, the most the line ever owned.

The Second World War was to prove the busiest time in the working of the Tramway. Portrush became an important evacuation centre for those who were escaping from Belfast following the Blitz of 1941. To save fuel, the Northern Ireland Road Transport Board withdrew bus services between Portrush and Bushmills, leaving the Tramway to provide a full all-the-year-round service (for a number of years it had become the practice to close for the winter). This was provided by the two saloon powercars (Nos 9 and 24) hauling saloon trailers.

In 1942, a large Army camp was established between Portballintrae and the Giant's Causeway with the Tramway being the only form of transport between this camp and the railhead at Portrush. To cope with this, even the open 'toast racks' had to be used. In order to provide some protection in winter, three of them were provided with glass fronts and canvas side screens.

In the late 1940's, life was beginning to return to normal with cars and petrol becoming more plentiful. Receipts began to fall and in 1949, the Tramway barely paid its way. The years had taken their toll and despite much remedial work in that year, more was needed, including wholesale re-laying of the track, new conductor wires and, most importantly, the provision of rheostatic brakes on the tramcars. It was estimated that this would cost £14,600. The money was not forthcoming, nor was there any offer of help from public or private funds, so the Tramway, which had closed for the winter on 30th September, 1949, failed to reopen.

An Abandonment Order was sought in September 1950 but was not issued until September 1951. The entire undertaking was sold by public auction on 15th September, 1951. The sale took 35 minutes and raised a total of £11,600, considerably less than the estimated cost of repair. Later sales of the buildings and site realised a further £4,000.

The building which housed the powerplant at Walkmills can still be seen, as can the station house at Bushmills, now a dwelling house. The line of track from the outskirts of Portrush is clearly visible as a footpath and most of the passing places can be identified. Even stumps of some of the trolley poles can still be seen.

The trackbed from Bushmills to the Giant's Causeway is intact, as is the site of the old terminus. This is, of course, to be the site of the new 'Giant's Causeway & Bushmills Railway'.

Two of the old tramcars, Saloon No. 2 and 'toast rack' No. 5, are on display in the Transport Gallery of the Ulster Folk & Transport Museum at Cultra, just outside Belfast, while a third tramcar, one of the powercars (No. 9), is undergoing restoration at the Irish National Transport Museum at Howth Castle, Co. Dublin.

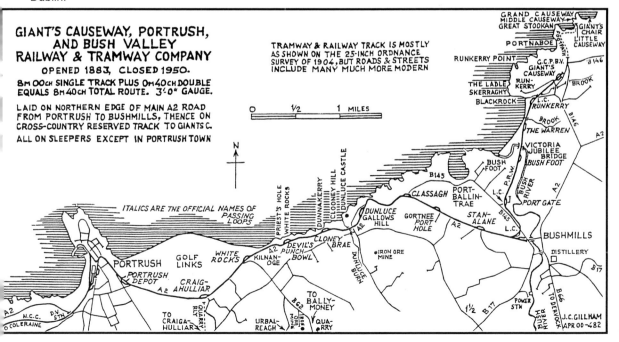

Portrush Harbour Branch in the nineteenth century.

(Lawrence Collection, courtesy of the National Library of Ireland)

We start our journey along the tramway with the little-used and short-lived branch to Portrush harbour. This can be seen clearly in the centre background curving down, through a run-round loop, to join the Belfast and Northern Counties Railway (B&NCR) branch to the harbour. From the junction, the laying of a third line of rails allowed traffic of either gauge (5ft 3in and 3ft) onwards to the harbour, where a coastal sailing ship is berthed. The branch was the preserve of the three steam tramway locomotives then in service and was intended to exploit the export of iron ore and limestone. This traffic never reached its potential and the Tramway ceased to use the line in June 1888.

A siding, to allow the interchange of goods between the Tramway and the B&NCR, diverged from the branch. Three of the Tramway's six tipping wagons can be seen after discharge of limestone into the wagons on the (Irish) standard gauge siding below. In the foreground, powercar No. 4 is sandwiched between two goods wagons in the terminus loop.

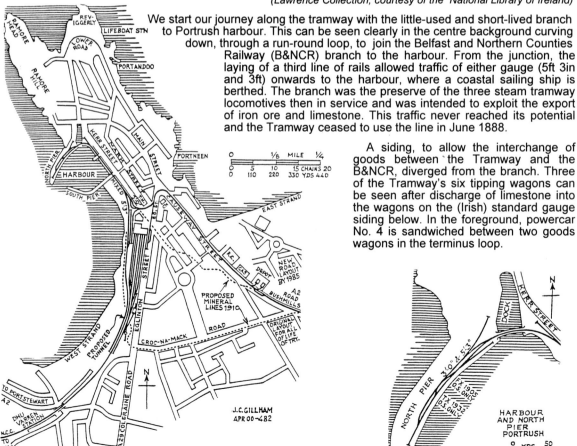

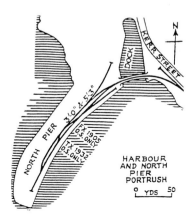

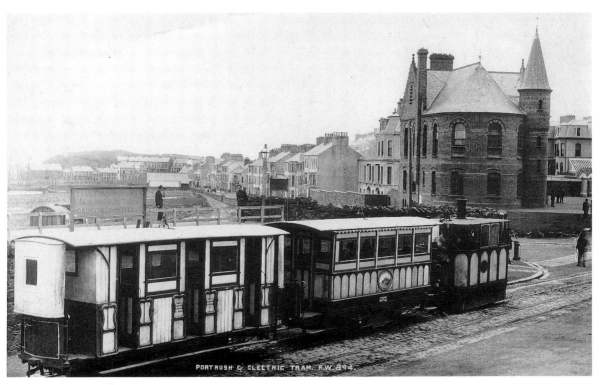

A steam locomotive hauling two powercars from Portrush station to the depot.

(Welch Collection, courtesy Ulster Museum)

Steam locomotive, No. 1 or No. 2, is leaving Portrush station hauling powercars Nos 4 & 7 during operation of the third rail. The Board of Trade forbade the use of the third rail in the town area, thus necessitating the use of steam traction between the station and the depot in Portrush. No. 7 was one of the original 'toast racks' fitted with a motor for third rail and also 'built-in' to provide shelter in winter. This photograph was taken before 1893, when the B&NCR station was rebuilt. Below, the same scene in the early 1930's shortly before the formation of the Northern Ireland Road Transport Board. The bus in the forecourt of the station is a Leyland LT2 belonging to the Northern Counties Railway. They only allowed their own buses in their forecourt. The bus outside the Town Hall is a Reo which belonged to Samuel S Henry who ran it between Portrush and Coleraine, via Portstewart. The cars in the station forecourt are taxis. Private cars were excluded from this area.

An electric tram departs the Portrush terminus.   *(From a Valentine postcard, Robin Linsley Collection)*

Steam supreme outside and inside the original Portrush station in the late nineteenth century.

(Lawrence Collection, courtesy of the National Library of Ireland)

Another good example of what a treasure house the Lawrence collection is for the student of railway history! Two steam tramway locomotives at Portrush prior to the introduction of the overhead wire. One is about to haul powercar No. 4 to the edge of town, from where it will make its way under its own power to the Causeway. The second locomotive is waiting for the first to leave so that it may complete its running round and then haul the second rake of cars, headed by powercar No. 3. A 'toast rack' trailer and two wagons sit on the harbour branch, while another is just visible with a limestone load on the interchange siding behind the standard gauge goods vans. A B&NCR locomotive has been turned on the turntable at the end of the platform ready for its return journey

Car No. 22 at Portrush terminus. *(From a Valentine postcard, Robin Linsley Collection)*

At the turn of the last century, in the early days of the overhead wire, one of the new 'toast rack' powercars No. 22 is running round at the station. Note the large crowd waiting to board. The B&NCR station had been rebuilt into architect Berkeley Deane Wise's mock-Tudor masterpiece in 1893 and at that time the tramway's runround loop was moved some 75 yards further down Eglinton Street. The time on the station clock indicates that it is early afternoon when most people would set off for the Causeway to allow enough time to return for their evening meal. After running round, a powercar is seen with one of the original six-bench 'toast rack' trailers and trailer No. 4, ready for its journey to the Causeway. The car's 'trolley' pole pick-up from the overhead wire is clearly visible. This system was invented and perfected in the USA, from which the Tramway obtained the necessary equipment. Note the horse-drawn sidecars which provided private conveyance in the days before taxis.

Portrush station in the early days of the overhead wire.

(From a contemporary postcard, Robin Linsley Collection)

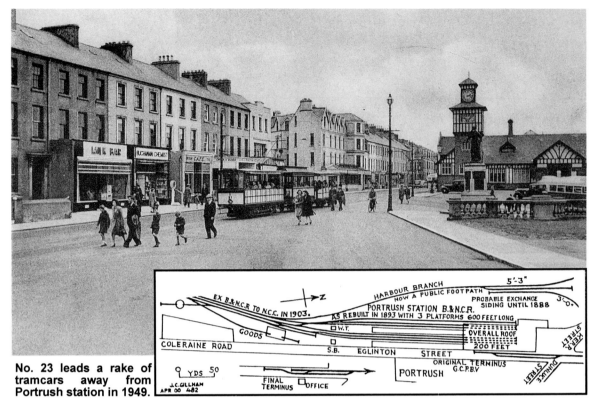

No. 23 leads a rake of tramcars away from Portrush station in 1949.

(From a contemporary postcard, Author's Collection)

During the last year of operation, No. 23, with trailer No. 10 and a 'toast rack' trailer, is leaving for the Causeway. Notice the almost complete absence of cars except for the taxis in the forecourt of the station, even though petrol rationing had ceased in 1947. It is interesting to observe the attire of the people in the picture. Even on a warm sunny day in 1949, which can be remembered for its particularly fine weather, they are rather formally dressed wearing their best clothes for the visit to the seaside.

A steam locomotive with five trailers, the maximum allowed by the Board of Trade, is leaving the station. Steam operation remained a necessity until the upgrading of the Portrush power plant in 1925. The horse-drawn omnibus belonged to the Northern Counties Hotel. The wealthy clients of the hotel were met and transported by this vehicle with its liveried attendants. The less wealthy made their way to their boarding houses by jaunting car, or on foot.

Having left the station, the tram proceeded along Eglinton Street.   *(Author's Collection)*

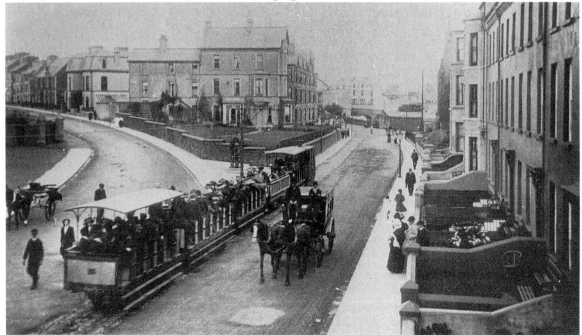

A steam-hauled tram proceeds down Eglinton Street .

(From a contemporary postcard, Robin Linsley Collection)

From Portrush station, the tramway continued along Eglinton Street and here a steam locomotive heads a rake of three trailers on a sunny day in the early 1920's. The newspaper placard proclaims a headline which might nearly be in place eighty years later, but by happier contrast the unsightly hoardings at the junction of Main Street and Causeway Street have gone.

No. 23, driven by James McFadden, with saloon and 'toast rack' trailers, rounds the 'Methodist Corner' and enters Causeway Street on a wet day in 1948. Note the Presbyterian Church in the background. Quite early on in the life of the Tramway, it was decided to have Sunday running, much to the annoyance of the local Church people. It is alleged that one Sunday the Minister, Rev. Simpson, was praying that "this evil desecration of the Sabbath would cease". During the prayer a tram rounded the corner with a noisy squealing of steel wheel against steel rail. The Minister is reported to have paused and looked to Heaven saying "Thou canst hear for Thyself, O Lord, the knell of their wickedness".

Car No. 23 takes the sharp corner into Causeway Street on an unseasonable day *(Author's Collection)*

Causeway Street, Portrush.

A steam-hauled tram in Causeway Street. *(From a Signal postcard, Robin Linsley Collection)*

An unidentified steam locomotive with one saloon and three 'toast rack' trailers makes its way along Causeway Street heading for the Causeway, in the very early years of last century. The last trailer appears to be No. 15, one of the five-bench 'toast racks' converted from goods wagons. Note the very formal dress of people out for their afternoon stroll. Tee-shirts, baseball caps and trainers were not the order of the day then!

No. 20 with saloon and 'toast rack' trailers enters the passing place at the depot at the bottom of Causeway Street. This was the point where the third rail commenced, prior to overhead operation. In times past, even towns of modest size had their own gasworks and Portrush was no exception. One assumes that the planners had hidden Portrush's well away from the genteel eyes of visitors, on the outskirts of town, only to have the Tramway offer them a perfect view!

The tramway left town just past the Gasworks and entered the first passing place at the Depot.

(Courtesy A.D. Packer)

A tram is posed at the Portrush Depot loop at the turn of the last century.
(Lawrence Collection, courtesy of the National Library of Ireland)

A view of Portrush depot in its original condition. The large building was the tramshed with the workshop to the left. They were built of basalt with sandstone quoins and were in existence until demolished recently to make way for a supermarket. To the right of the main building was the steam locomotive shed. It was much less elaborate and was removed when steam traction ended and the new power plant was installed in 1925. The steam locomotive with five trailers is making its way to the Causeway. There are no powercars in the rake, which would be too heavy for electric traction.

A steam-hauled tram, including a goods wagon passes the Depot.

(Lawrence Collection, courtesy of the National Library of Ireland)

A steam tramway locomotive with a loaded goods wagon, a saloon trailer and two 'toast rack' trailers passes Portrush depot. This train will proceed under steam power as it is much too heavy for electric traction. The inclusion of a goods wagon is unusual, as goods traffic was sparse and never met expectations.

Below, a steam locomotive with four 'toast rack' trailers and saloon No. 9 passing Portrush Golf Course in the very early days of overhead power. No. 9 was given a new chassis and motors and converted to a powercar for overhead working in 1908. The second passing place, Craigahulliar, was beside the links which later became 'The Royal Portrush Golf Club', an international course where the British Open, won by Max Faulkner, was played in the late 1950's. This was the only time the competition was played in Ireland. The Seniors British Open Championship is now played here on a regular basis and it retains its reputation as one of the world's most testing courses.

A steam locomotive and a rake of trailers passing the Golf Club on its way to Portrush.

(Welch Collection, courtesy Ulster Museum)

A tram beyond the White Rocks where the sea was just behind the wall. *(Author's Collection)*

Beyond the White Rocks passing place, the tramway ran alongside the cliffs overlooking the sea where the scenery was magnificent. Here No. 20 with two trailers is leaving the section at the White Rocks. The passengers had an excellent view over the wall to the sea and rocks below.

No. 23 with trailers waiting to meet a tram at the crossing place at Devil's Punchbowl (Priest's Hole). There were a total of fourteen passing places (or 'loops') on the route where trams met in a pre-determined pattern. In this picture the crew of driver, Robbie Jamison, and the conductor, the author, are waiting for a tram coming from Portrush.

For the entire length of the track there were two overhead wires. A tram from Portrush to the Causeway used the wire next to the sea and always travelled on the inside, or sea-side, track at a loop. A tram in the opposite direction, however, invariably used the outside wire and the outside track. The points were set to allow this procedure and were spring-loaded to permit a tram to leave a loop without changing them. The spring reset the points after the tram had passed.

A Portrait of the Author as a Young Man; Devil's Punch Bowl Loop, 1949.

(Harry Twiss, Author's Collection)

Car No. 20 approaching the summit between Devil's Punch Bowl and Dunluce.

(W.A.Camwell, courtesy Stephenson Locomotive Society)

The line proceeded from the Devil's Punchbowl to the summit near Dunluce. No. 20 and trailers are climbing the hill to the summit. The island just visible is one of the 'Skerries' chain.

A view from the tram as it made its way along the top of the cliffs with the white limestone rocks clearly visible. These rocks had many features, the most famous being 'The Giant's Head' seen below here. The controls of the powercar are evident, the controller on the left and the handbrake on the right. This was the only means of stopping a tram, short of throwing the controller into reverse! Needless to say, this latter method was officially frowned upon and staff were lectured on the likely resulting damage to the electrical equipment of the tram. Of course, speeds seldom exceeded 15mph, but the need for better brakes was to be a contributing factor to closure.

A driver's and passengers' view from the tram between the White Rocks and Dunluce.

(Author's Collection)

Waiting patiently at the passing loop at Cloney Brae. *(Author's Collection)*

No. 23 with trailers waiting at the Cloney Brae passing place near the summit in 1949, the last year of running. This photograph gives a good view of the lateral seating on the 'toast racks' which were very pleasant to travel on in fine weather. Note that in good weather the saloon was empty.

The tramway was often used for special excursions. On 25th April, 1942 it was hired by Queen's University Belfast, to transport a party of students from the School of Civil Engineering and the School of Geology on a geological outing. The geology of this area has always been of great interest to those who study the subject. Apart from the Causeway, which is one of the most famous geological features of the world, the area has a wide variety of rocks in all groups. The students helped to push the tram over the summit.

A helping hand to get the tram over the summit. *(Jackson McCormick, Author's Collection)*

Classic Dunluce - An original electric car passing.

A most attractive view of powercar No. 4 with trailer passing Dunluce in the days of the third rail. A superb model of these two cars, along with others, is on display in the Fry Museum at Malahide Castle, Co. Dublin.

(Lawrence Collection, courtesy of the National Library of Ireland)

This and the later photograph of Bushmills station *(page 24)* illustrate how potentially dangerous the third rail was and there were many accidents with it. Things came to a head following a fatal accident in August 1895 when a cyclist struck the kerb alongside the line and fell across the third rail. The unfortunate man died at Bushmills station half-an-hour later.

At the coroner's inquest a dispute arose as to whether the man died from electrocution or concussion. Mr Traill maintained that it was not electrocution and, to prove his point, agreed to sit on the live third rail without trousers. A demonstration was arranged at the Golf Course and Mr Traill, in order to show that the line was live, arranged for a tram to pass the assembled party. As it climbed the hill to the White Rocks he removed his trousers and sat on the rail in full view of the party. He did not point out to them that the tram was between him and the power station nor did he tell them that another tram was climbing the hill out of Bushmills at the same time, leaving virtually no power at the location of the demonstration. He also overlooked telling them that he was wearing especially heavy-duty insulated boots. He then challenged his opponents to sit on the rail but they declined. There are many versions of this story but this is the one given by Mr Traill's widow to the author when he worked there in 1949. She was the last Managing Director of the Tramway.

Steam tramway locomotive with passenger trailers and goods wagon passing Dunluce.

(Author's Collection)

A very rare view of goods haulage. A link to Portrush harbour was constructed and there were various plans to convey iron ore for export. However, the goods wagons purchased at the time of the opening were seldom used and after this traffic was abandoned in 1893 all were converted to 'toast rack' trailers. It is probable that the coal in the wagon was for the Tramway's own use, as a steam locomotive was stationed at Bushmills to deal with the branch to the town.

A pleasing study of a steam tramway locomotive hauling a 'toast rack' and saloon trailer in the days of the third rail. Despite the fact that the locomotive could be driven from either end, the drivers appear to have made a practice of driving from the end with the firebox door, so that they could tend to the fire, while on the move. Thus they would normally be at the front for one journey and the rear for the other. The first trailer is one of the converted goods wagons where the 'toast rack' was set on top of the wagon and the two floors are clearly visible. The photographer has taken this view from a slightly different angle from that normally favoured, so that the Skerries are visible out to sea.

A steam-hauled tram passing Dunluce Castle.

(Lawrence Collection, courtesy of the National Library of Ireland)

An original electric powercar leading a 'toast rack' trailer from the Giant's Causeway terminus.
(Lawrence Collection, courtesy of the National Library of Ireland)

This panoramic view shows the Giant's Causeway buildings as they were in the late 1890's. The two hotels are shown clearly; the one on the right has been demolished but the one on the left, The Causeway Hotel, is still in existence. The building in the centre is the old Causeway visitors centre and café, which remained long after the Tramway closed. It was replaced by a modern building some years ago.

HOTELS GIANTS CAUSEWAY. 5548. W.L

In the foreground is the terminus with the 'Pagoda' in the centre. This was the waiting room and was brought all the way from Switzerland at a cost of £400. The small building to the left of the Pagoda is the water tower for steam locomotives and on the right, behind the fence, was a small shop and refreshment room.

The tram leaving the terminus was one of the saloon power cars, No. 2, towing a small 'toast rack' trailer in the days of the third rail.

Even the skill of Lawrence's photographer, Robert French, could not bring the tramway and the basalt columns, for which the Causeway is famous, into the same view. They are just round the corner of the headland.

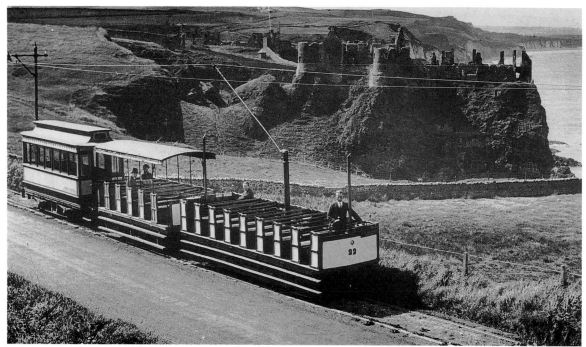

One of the 'toast rack' powercars in original condition with a typical tram. *(Courtesy Belfast Newsletter)*

A 1937 view of 'toast rack' powercar No. 22 as originally built in 1902. The 'overhead' powercars were built without roofs but these were fitted to three of them shortly afterwards, due to the danger from broken trolley poles. Fortunately no-one was injured but the risk was obvious. No. 22 was the exception as it was only used in times of peak traffic. Below is a similar view taken during the last year of operation. The almost empty tram indicates the reason for closure. Both these photographs show the typical layout of a rake of cars and, where possible, a saloon was included in each rake.

Dunluce Castle, one of the most famous in Ireland, was built in the late 1300's by the Norman Earl of Ulster, Richard de Burgh. It occupied an almost impenetrable position, perched on top of a cliff with the only entrance being a wooden drawbridge across a deep ravine. There was an escape route to a cave below, only accessible by boat. It had a very turbulent history being occupied by a number of families including the O'Neills, the MacQuillans and the MacDonnells. Part of it was swept into the sea in a fierce storm in 1639 with a considerable loss of life and it was abandoned shortly after.

A common scene in the later years of the Tramway. *(Contemporary postcard, Robin Linsley Collection)*

DUNLUCE CASTLE AND THE PORTRUSH CAUSEWAY TRAM.

Tram waiting at passing place at Portballintrae Road.   *(Author's Collection)*

From Dunluce, the line continued past Classagh loop to that known as Port Hole. This was the first of two stops convenient for Portballintrae. A rake of tramcars is waiting at the passing place with Portballintrae Road just in front. It is waiting for a tram climbing the hill from Bushmills.

This is the location of an incident which made the Tramway go down in history as the only Irish railway or tramway to suffer damage at the hands of the Germans during the First World War. On 16th May, 1916 an armed coaster, the *Wheatear*, while sailing from Coleraine to England, was attacked by a German submarine which was on the surface. The coaster fought back and eventually escaped to shelter behind the Skerries. During the battle, which lasted 2½ hours, about 250 shells were fired, some of which damaged the overhead poles and wires. By a strange coincidence, the Wheatear's sister ship was sunk by another surfaced U-boat off Wales.

Saloon powercar No. 9 in its pre-war state, with two trailers, climbing the long hill from Bushmills towards Portrush. This climb was known as the Stana Lane and included the passing place of that name.

Car No. 9 climbs the hill near Stana Lane.   *(W.A.Camwell, courtesy Stephenson Locomotive Society)*

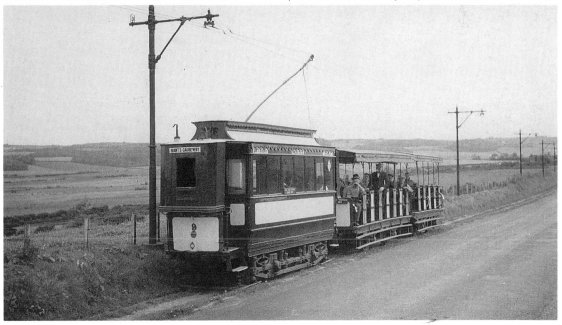

An early view of Bushmills station in the days of the third rail. *(Author's Collection)*

The station building at Bushmills was a large structure and the only one of its type on the line. Had the plan for the line to Dervock become a reality, Bushmills would have become the 'Grand Junction' of the system. The station, which boasted a Station Master, is still in existence as a dwelling house and appears to be in pristine condition. The rake consists of powercar No. 4 and a trailer. Note a pick-up at each end of the powercar and one at the end of the trailer. This allowed the tram to cross gaps at road junctions, lanes and field entrances. The potential danger of the third rail is again well illustrated.

A view of Bushmills Station at a much later date, in the time of overhead operation. The buildings on the right are the sheds where some trams were stored at night. The line in the foreground led to the Bushmills market place and was, of course, steam-worked. If the original plans had been realised, it would have marked the start of the line to Dervock. The White House is a departmental store in Portrush, popular with visitors. Its advertising hoardings were a prominent feature at several places along the line.

An overall view of the Bushmills station area in the days of the overhead wire.

(H.R.Norman: L&GRP/NRM)

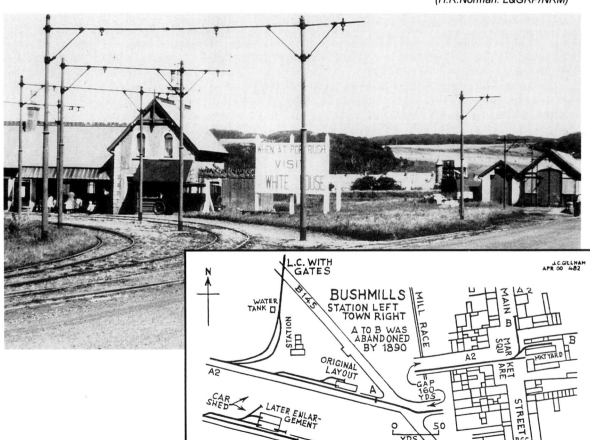

A tram crossing the Victoria Jubilee Bridge in the latter years of the Tramway. *(Courtesy A.D.Packer)*

The original tramway ended at Bushmills, from which the line was extended as a railway, in its own right of way, opening in 1887. From Bushmills, the extension continued through the Port Gate loop, a second point of access to Portballintrae and the one at Bush Foot. This was just before the only major engineering feature on the Tramway, 'The Victoria Jubilee Bridge', opened in 1887, the year of the Queen's Golden Jubilee.

The bridge was roughly half-way between Bushmills and the terminus and had three spans, one 70ft and two 22ft. The views show a tram crossing it heading towards Bushmills, and a driver's view of the bridge, travelling towards the sand dunes. The bridge deck became dangerous in the 1970's and was removed by the Army, later to be replaced by a footbridge erected by the local District Council, who were constructing a footpath along the line of the old track. This footbridge has since been removed and is being replaced as part of the revived railway.

A driver's view as the tram crossed the bridge, heading for the sand dunes.

(Courtesy Ulster Folk and Transport Museum)

The final length of track ran behind Runkerry Strand. *(Author's Collection)*

The final stretch of line included loops at The Warren and Runkerry. This view shows the route along the sandhills behind the strand, with Runkerry House in the background. This portion of line is the site of the new 'Giant's Causeway & Bushmills Railway'.

Below, a very busy scene at the Causeway terminus with a steam-hauled tram ready to leave. There are eight uniformed staff in the picture and it is probable that there are two or more trams at the terminus. One of the problems with the Tramway, at busy times, was to ensure that all the passengers who travelled out to the Causeway got home. Even in the last year this proved to be a problem. Some people went out in the morning and spent a whole day at the Causeway whereas others went out after lunch for a half day. A man was employed to count the passengers arriving at the Causeway and those who had left by mid afternoon. If necessary, extra trams would be provided in the evening. Note the water stand-pipe feeding from the water tower behind the locomotive.

Steam engine with a rake of heavily loaded trailers about to depart from the Giant's Causeway.

(Author's Collection)

Giant's Causeway terminus in third rail days with Lawrence's photographer, Robert French, waiting to return to Portrush. *(Lawrence Collection, courtesy of the National Library of Ireland)*

No. 9, in its original third rail form, sits outside the Pagoda at the terminus, complete with 'toast rack' trailer, waiting to return to Portrush. The tram is above the points for the loop. On arrival, it would have run round and reversed at speed past the third rail to allow another tram to enter the station. The third rail is just visible beside the Pagoda at the left of the picture. The gentleman sitting on the seat is Lawrence's photographer, Robert French, who took most of the Lawrence photographs in the north of the island of Ireland and those around Portrush. His equipment sits on the bench and some of his photographs include the jaunting car, which carried him and his equipment.

On a fine sunny day, the late Henry Casserley's ubiquitous camera captured powercar No. 21, with 'toast rack' and saloon trailers awaiting passengers. The brake handles are prominent at each end, but the absent driver has, of course, removed the controller handle! A fully loaded No. 20 with 'toast rack' and saloon trailers is about to depart. As it leaves, it will pass No. 21 using the outside line and overhead wire. No. 21 will then reverse and change trolley wire ready to depart. Both powercars are in their original condition with the supports for the trolley pole clearly visible.

The building on the crown of the hill was once a combined Church of Ireland Church and Schoolhouse, built in 1915 by the MacNaghten family to a design by the architect Clough Williams-Ellis, the creator of the famous Portmeirion village in North Wales. As a church it was used for a relatively short time, but continued as a primary school until quite recently. It is now the 'Causeway School Museum' portraying school life during the early part of the last century.

Waiting for the Rush Hour 10th August, 1920. *(H.C. Casserley)*

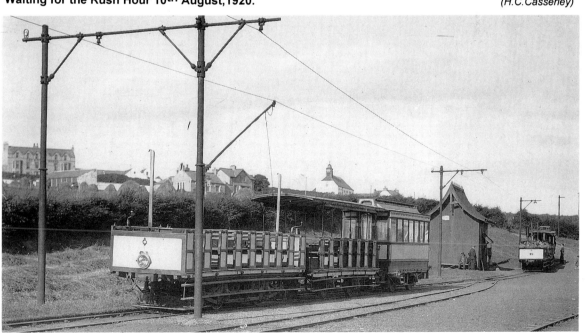

Steam hauled tram awaits passengers at the Causeway terminus.

(L&GRP/NRM)

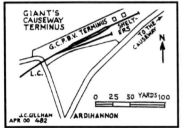

This siding was for steam only and was never provided with a third rail or overhead wires. In latter years it could be used at busy times to store a waiting tram by towing it from the other lines with a long chain, a very dangerous practice. The steam locomotive is either No. 1 or No. 2. The first trailer is the old powercar No. 4; the second is interesting as it is the only known photograph of a 'toast rack' with the open side next to the sea and being a six-bench car, is one of the original cars Nos 5-8; the rear trailer is old powercar No. 3. One can just see where the 'pick-ups' for the third rail have been removed from the former and latter.

No. 20 runs round its trailers at the terminus in preparation for its return journey to Portrush. The reader might be confused by the need for an electric unit to have to run round its train, as to-day it could be controlled from a driving cab in a vehicle at either end. However, the technology to control a powercar from a driving position in a trailer had not been perfected when these cars were built. Thus, the Tramway's powercars acted like locomotives and had to run round their trailers at each end of the journey.

Car No. 20 runs round her train of trailers at the terminus.   *(Courtesy A.D.Packer)*

Car No. 22 leads her train out of the terminus. *(Robin Linsley Collection)*

No. 22 with trailers is seen leaving the terminus in the 1930's. The points in front of the tram appear to be set against it, being set for the 'inside' track. However, the points are spring-loaded and will spring across to allow the tram to pass, reverting to their normal position to allow the next tram entering the terminus to proceed along the inside track. The steam siding is clearly evident on the right hand side of the picture.

No. 9, in its final form, leaves the terminus with the conductor commencing his ticket collection. As an ex-conductor, the author can assure the reader that this was a job that required great skill climbing along the side of each car and, like a monkey, hopping from one to the next while doing his ticket round. Falls led to several conductors losing a leg and one wonders what the present 'Health and Safety Executive' would have to say about this dangerous practice. Behind No. 9 is No. 24 waiting its turn. Beyond the run-round loop is a length of track sufficiently long to hold a powercar and two trailers. No. 24 was a spare car, only used at busy times, and is probably waiting for the evening rush. Note how dilapidated the surroundings have become towards the end due to lack of funds.

Car No. 9 leaves the terminus in the late 1940s. *(Author's Collection)*

Changing the trolley pole to permit the powercar to run round at Portrush Station.

(Author's Collection)

These two views show features of the Tramway in operation. No. 23 is running round its trailers at Portrush station in preparation for a return journey to the Causeway. Running round with overhead wires was quite a complicated business with the trolley pole being changed at each change of direction, three times in the manoeuvre. In this photograph, taken in 1949, the driver is Robbie Jamison and the conductor, the author.

Climbing aboard a 'toast rack' was not for the weak or fainthearted as is shown here at the Causeway terminus, another feature which would not find favour to-day. However each rake of cars normally had a saloon with much easier access.

Car No. 20 loading at the Giant's Causeway. *(Author's Collection)*

In 1925 an oil engine replaced an earlier gas one at Portrush depot to improve the provision of electric power. The depot building was extended to house this engine as shown in the top picture. This extension was built of basalt with sandstone quoins to match the existing building.

The centre picture shows the inside of the powerhouse. *(both Author's Collection)*

The bottom picture shows Walkmills hydro-electric power station in its early days, prior to reconstruction in 1900. It shows how the River Bush dropped over the Salmon Leap here, while the station harnessed the river's power by means of a head race some 200 yards long from a weir built across the river upstream.

(Welch Collection, courtesy Ulster Museum)

Bushmills tramshed with adjoining shed for the Tramway's donkey. *(Author's Collection)*

The tramshed at Bushmills held two rakes of cars, one powercar and two trailers each. One of the rakes did the early morning service, starting at Bushmills and transporting people to work in Portrush. This set and crew finished work at tea time. The second set commenced work at mid-day, before the busy afternoon, and finished late at night bringing people home to Bushmills after an evening's entertainment.

The tramshed only had an overhead power line to one road, the second road being known locally as the 'dead road'. A tram was taken out of the shed using a long electrical trailing lead until it reached the other road and could be connected to the overhead supply. The lead was live and simply plugged into a power point in the depot; the other end was connected to the tramcar, just as one would use a long extension lead for a power tool, except that the lead was very heavy and carried 550 volts! The tram which the author worked on was stored overnight in this tramshed and he assisted in this operation each morning.

The third road led to what was once a steam shed and could be used for storage, using the trailing lead. The small shed to the left of the main shed was a donkey house. Bushmills was the nearest station to the seaside resort of Portballintrae, which had two hotels and a couple of boarding houses. Passengers for the resort had their luggage transported by the Tramway donkey.

Car No. 22 with a rake of cars in Bushmills siding. *(Author's Collection)*

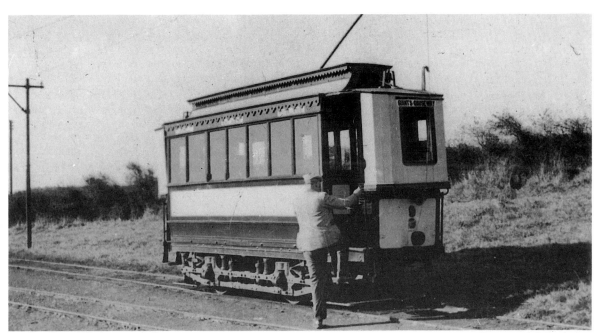

No. 9 on Winter service. *(Courtesy A.D.Packer)*

No. 9, before its final rebuild in 1945, is seen at the Causeway terminus. It is probably operating a winter service during the Second World War. Prior to and after the War, the Tramway operated from May to September, closing for the winter. The Act of Parliament, authorising its inauguration, stipulated that it must run a full service and, to comply with this regulation, a tram ran a single service, once a month, complete with conductor and money bag.

Below, powercar No. 21 in its final state, with trailer No. 2, is at the Giant's Causeway terminus in 1948. During the Second World War the Tramway was extremely busy and had to press into service the open 'toast racks'. Three of them, Nos 20, 21 & 23 were fitted with glass fronts and canvas side screens which could be let down in wet weather to give some protection.

The Tramway had a staff of 26 the last year it ran; 6 of these were full-time staff who worked the whole year round and carried out maintenance functions in the winter. The remaining 20 were part-time and worked for the summer season only. The conductor in this photograph is Willie Montgomery, who was one of the full-time staff and, as well as driving or conducting, he was Station Master at Bushmills, living in the Station House and looking after the station. The driver was Davy Godfrey, who was one of the part-time staff. Davy had a small farm and, in his early days, was a scutcher in Ballybogey Scutch Mill. Men like Davy worked on the Tramway in summer and had a different job for winter.

No. 21 with a saloon trailer at the Causeway. *(Author's Collection)*

Saloon Trailers at the Causeway.

A line-up of trailers, in fact the entire saloon fleet together with one 'toast rack' at the Causeway terminus. The drawbar in front of the first car suggests that it is connected to a steam tramway locomotive. The saloons were a masterpiece of the coachmaker's art with carved valancing under the clerestory roof and gutter, the panelled sides decorated with the Tramway's crest and the ornate wrought iron gates on the entrance balcony, where the handle of the brake is visible. All trailers were provided with a brake, although only for parking purposes.

The sign advertises the Causeway Hotel which is directly above the terminus, but out of view to the left here. The photographer has contrived to place the main building of Kane's Royal Hotel behind the competitor's sign! The former hotel was supplied with electric power by the Tramway company and the post with a cross, to the left of the waiting room, marks the start of the power line. For this amenity, the hotel paid just £10 a year, when the arrangement was first made in 1889.

(Lawrence Collection, courtesy of the National Library of Ireland)

34

No. 24 outside Portrush Station on Winter service. *(Author's Collection)*

The 'Dunfermline Tram' sits outside Portrush station in September 1949, the last month of operation. This car was the only one with a heater which made it very popular in the winter. It was originally an open top double-decker of 3ft 6in gauge. On arrival at Portrush it was re-gauged and the top deck removed. The chassis was the same as the remaining powercars.

That prolific photographer, Ken Nunn, chose a wet day for his only visit to the Tramway in the 1920s. His record of open topped powercar No. 21 with a 'toast rack' trailer shows how the trailer seats were protected by a canvas cover to keep the seats dry. These covers were later replaced by roll-up canvas screens. When the tram set off, one side of the screen was removed, depending on which way the wind and rain were blowing. At such times, the powercar would have been avoided by most passengers, but the unfortunate driver had to brave the elements. This apparent disregard for the comfort of the staff (and passengers!) was common in Victorian times when the car was built. Even the driving cabs of railway locomotives only became properly enclosed in the twentieth century. Clearly our ancestors were a hardier people!

No. 21 and 'toast rack' trailer outside Portrush Station on a wet day.
(Ken Nunn, courtesy of Locomotive Club of Great Britain)

Open 'toast rack' Trailer. *(Author's Collection)*

These views at the Portrush depot allow a closer study of the Tramway's trailers. No. 7 was typical of the 'toast rack' trailers used. These fell into three groups and were easily identifiable. The first group, Nos 5-8, were six-bench cars and date from the opening of the Tramway, or very soon after. The second group, Nos 11-17, were five-bench cars. They were converted from goods wagons and had two bodies, the 'toast rack' being simply set on top of the wagon. The third set consisted of two cars, Nos 18 & 19, which were seven-bench cars, purchased in 1897.

Following the end of the third rail, open powercars Nos 3 & 4 were converted to trailers. Some attempts were made to convert No. 4 to overhead electrical pick-up but these were unsuccessful and soon abandoned. No. 4 had a roof and lasted until closure but No. 3, which had been out of use for some time and did not have a roof, was cannibalised in 1945 to refurbish No. 9. Here No. 4 still retained all its delightful Victorian features.

Converted powercar. *(Author's Collection)*

Tramway Locomotive showing how the 'skirts' might be raised for maintenance.

(H.R.Norman: L&GRP/NRM)

There were four tramway locomotives and photographs of Nos 1 and 2 appear earlier. From views in contemporary postcards, they appear to have been painted Tuscan red and cream. Both were withdrawn early in the twentieth century. All four locomotives came from Wilkinson's and were of similar design having vertical boilers and an 0-4-0 wheel arrangement.

The later two, however, continued in use until the mid-1920s, the precise date of their last use on the Tramway is unclear, but probably as late as 1926. In 1931, they were sold to Mr Faris, who was building a breakwater at the mouth of the River Bann. They were recorded on 15th July, 1933 during this second period of their working lives. Their eventual fate remains a mystery.

The locomotive above is No. 4 Brian Boroimhe (Brian Boru) during this period. The cab has been removed and the 'side skirts' are raised suggesting that it is under repair. These skirts were to provide protection to the general public and animals from the moving parts of the engine. This was a legal requirement for all tramway locomotives which, of course, usually ran along (or alongside) public roads, as did the 'tramway' section between Portrush and Bushmills.

Sister locomotive No. 3 Dunluce Castle is seen while working on the breakwater project also and may be at the quarry which provided the stone. Both appear to retain the dark green livery in which they were painted in later Tramway days.

No. 3 at work by the River Bann.

(H.R.Norman: L&GRP/NRM)

Works wagon built on steam locomotive No. 1. *(Author's Collection)*

The Tramway was never a prosperous affair and only survived due to the good housekeeping of Mr Traill and his successors. An example of this is shown here, where a body from one of the goods wagons, converted to a 'toast rack' trailer, was fitted to the chassis of steam locomotive No. 1 which had been withdrawn in 1908. This vehicle, which shows clearly the chassis and axles of the steam locomotive, lasted as a permanent way wagon until closure. The wagon is standing beside the tower wagon, used for maintenance of the overhead wire and is sitting on the sidings which formerly led to the steam locomotive shed

The very sad picture below shows the breaking-up of the tramcars following the auction on 15th September, 1951. Of the group shown, No. 5 trailer was the only one to survive and is now on display at The Ulster Folk and Transport Museum at Cultra.

Demolition of vehicles at Portrush Depot. *(Author's Collection)*

Inside the depot and workshops.

A view of the inside of Portrush depot with tramcars in storage or under repair. The Tramway, like all similar undertakings, had to be completely self sufficient and carry out all its own repairs and maintenance.

Following the sale of the Tramway the demolition contractor broke up the tramcars salvaging all the metal for scrap. Many of the bodies became garden sheds or hen-houses. The body of No. 9 found its way to Youghal in County Cork, as the property of a local lady, Miss Nellie Mahir, who used it as a holiday home and a teashop. When Miss Mahir died in 1981, the tramcar was rescued and is now undergoing restoration in The Transport Museum of Ireland, Howth Castle, Co Dublin. Here it is being used as a teashop.

No. 9 as a teashop on Youghal Strand, Co.Cork.

GIANT'S CAUSEWAY AND PORTRUSH ELECTRIC TRAMWAY
WORLD'S FIRST HYDRO ELECTRIC TRAMWAY — OPENED IN 1883

TIME TABLE from 6th JULY, 1949
UNTIL FURTHER NOTICE

Tramcars between Portrush, Bushmills and Giant's Causeway will run as follows:—

WEEK DAYS			SUNDAYS		
Portrush to Bushmills and Giant's Causeway	Giant's Causeway to Bushmills and Portrush	Bushmills to Portrush	Portrush to Bushmills and Giant's Causeway	Giant's Causeway to Bushmills and Portrush	Bushmills to Portrush
10.30 a.m.	—	8.15 a.m.	10.30 a.m.	—	9.45 a.m.
11.20 ,,	9.45 ,,	9.45 ,,	12. 0 noon	—	10.45 ,,
12.45 p.m.	—	10.30 ,,	1.10 p.m.	—	11.45 ,,
1.30 ,,	11.20 a.m.	11.30 ,,	2.10 ,,	12.15 p.m.	12.25 p.m.
2.10 ,,	12.20 p.m.	12.30 p.m.	2.40 ,,	1. 0 ,,	1.10 ,,
2.40 ,,	1.35 ,,	1.45 ,,	3.10 ,,	2. 0 ,,	2.10 ,,
3.10 ,,	2.20 ,,	2.30 ,,	3.50 ,,	3. 0 ,,	3.10 ,,
3.40 ,,	3. 0 ,,	3.10 ,,	4.30 ,,	4. 0 ,,	4.10 ,,
4.10 ,,	4. 0 ,,	4.10 ,,	5.15 ,,	4.45 ,,	4.55 ,,
5.15 ,,	4.45 ,,	4.55 ,,	6. 0 ,,	5. 0 ,,	5.10 ,,
6. 0 ,,	5. 0 ,,	5.10 ,,	6.30 ,,	5.30 ,,	5.40 ,,
6.40 ,,	6.10 ,,	6.20 ,,	7.15 ,,	6.10 ,,	6.20 ,,
7.10 ,,	7. 0 ,,	7.10 ,,	X8.15 ,,	7.20 ,,	7.30 ,,
8. 0 ,,	8. 0 ,,	8.10 ,,			
X9. 0 ,,	—	—			
X—Bushmills only			X—Bushmills only		

SPECIAL EXCURSION TICKETS
Will be issued from Bushmills to Portrush Daily by all Tramcars at fare of 1/2 Return, available for day of issue only.

SUBSCRIPTION MONTHLY AND WEEKLY TICKETS
Are issued at Reduced Rates, also. Special Rates for School Children and Special Parties, on application to Tramway Office, Portrush. Special Tramcars can be engaged on application.

Travel by Electric Tramcars, the best means of viewing the beautiful coast and enjoying the magnificent scenery.

NOTE.—This Time Table is liable to alteration, if found necessary without notice from the Company.

The Company will not hold themselves responsible for Tramcars not starting at the times appointed, nor for delays that may occur on the road.

The Cars have special stopping places, indicated by sign, "CARS STOP HERE." Passengers are requested to meet the Cars at those places and are cautioned not to get on or off the Cars while in motion.

FARES

			Single Fare		*Return Fare	
Portrush and	Giant's Causeway		1s	9d	3s	0d
,,	,,	Bushmills ...	1s	0d	1s	6d
,,	,,	Dunluce Castle ...		9d	1s	0d
,,	,,	Portballintrae ...		10d	1s	3d
Bushmills and	Dunluce Castle ...			9d	1s	0d
,,	,,	Giant's Causeway		6d		
Portrush and	White Rocks ...			6d		
,,	,,	Golf Club ...		3d		

* Return Tickets are available for One Month from day of issue.

G. F. MEARA, Engineer/Manager.

Portrush, 6th July, 1949.

Telephone: Portrush 2318.

ITINERARY

The Tramway runs along the verge of the cliffs, skirting the blue waters of the North Atlantic for almost the entire distance to the Causeway.

Leaving Portrush the line rises by a gentle gradient to the White Rocks, where a magnificent view is obtained.

To the westward rise Innishowen and Malin Head, while the Skerries lie in the foreground, with the Island of Islay, off the Scottish coast, on the horizon.

The coast line is a succession of beautiful caves worn out by the waves of the Atlantic. Further along, at the Punch Bowl, where a sharp curve in the Tramway Track occurs, one can look down into the so-called Cathedral Cave.

A little further eastward is the Giant's Head, a gigantic profile in the white limestone rock, with a small crown of black basalt on its head.

The next siding affords a glimpse of a charming bay with the "Lion's Paw," a narrow ridge, running seaward, and the Wishing Arch, a perfect white limestone arch, spanning the deep blue water.

The summit, at 193 feet above sea level, is reached at Clooney Hill.

The next point of interest is Dunluce Castle, standing isolated on a projecting spur of basalt. This ancient stronghold of the MacQuillans has lately been taken over by the Northern Government, scheduled as an "ancient monument" and partially restored.

A mile farther along, below the Tramway line and close to the sea, lies Portballintrae, a small but favourite watering-place with excellent bathing and angling.

Bushmills is next passed, famous for its whiskey. Here, about three-quarters of a mile from the town, on the banks of the River Bush, amid charming surroundings, is situated the Hydro Electric Generating Station which supplies the Electricity to the Tramway.

Visitors to the district are cordially invited to visit this station, the first in the world to use "the waste waters of a river" to generate electricity for traction purposes and thereby gaining for the Tramway the distinction of being the Pioneer Hydro Electric Tramway of the World.

A pleasant run through the sand-hills now brings the traveller to the Giant's Causeway.

"There is nothing in the world like the Giant's Causeway," where "the rocks are cut as by a mathematical calculation." Most of the pillars are six-sided, some have five sides, a few four sides, fewer still have three and seven sides, and only one, the "Key Stone," has eight sides.

In the "Wishing Chair," the "Giant's Organ," the "Giant's Loom" and the "Honeycomb," to mention only a few examples, the sections of the pillars can best be seen. The "Giant's Well" always gives a constant flow of deliciously cool and sparkling water.

Famous also are the Causeway caves, one of them measuring 700 feet long with a height of 60 feet

Select Bibliography

Those wishing to learn more about the Tramway cannot do better than to read the late "Mac" McGuigan's excellent history - **The Giant's Causeway Tramway** (Oakwood, 1964). A new edition, bringing the story up to date, is in preparation.

The Tramway was the subject of an extensive article in the **Railway Magazine** of *May 1936* and is well described in Harold Fayle's classic **Narrow Gauge Railways of Ireland** (Greenlake, 1946). For the Tramway's place within the overall history of electric railways one may refer to **Age of the Electric Train** by J.C.Gillham (Ian Allan, 1988). Several recent general albums on the Irish railways include some fine pictures of the Tramway in action. The generation and use of electricity on the Tramway may be studied further in **History of Water Power in Ulster** by H.D.Gribbon (David & Charles, 1969).